Learning to Read, Step by Step!

Ready to Read   **Preschool–Kindergarten**
• big type and easy words • rhyme and rhythm • picture clues
For children who know the alphabet and are eager to begin reading.

Reading with Help   **Preschool–Grade 1**
• basic vocabulary • short sentences • simple stories
For children who recognize familiar words and sound out new words with help.

Reading on Your Own   **Grades 1–3**
• engaging characters • easy-to-follow plots • popular topics
For children who are ready to read on their own.

Reading Paragraphs   **Grades 2–3**
• challenging vocabulary • short paragraphs • exciting stories
For newly independent readers who read simple sentences with confidence.

Ready for Chapters   **Grades 2–4**
• chapters • longer paragraphs • full-color art
For children who want to take the plunge into chapter books but still like colorful pictures.

STEP INTO READING® is designed to give every child a successful reading experience. The grade levels are only guides; children will progress through the steps at their own speed, developing confidence in their reading.

Remember, a lifetime love of reading starts with a single step!

To Mom and Dad, who got us off to a great start on a lifetime of creature adventures
—M.K. and C.K.

For Xander and Gryphon
—R.W.

The authors would like to thank Kaitlin Dupuis for her help in creating this book.

Visit us on the Web!
StepIntoReading.com
rhcbooks.com

Educators and librarians, for a variety of teaching tools, visit us at
RHTeachersLibrarians.com

ISBN 978-0-593-37316-3 (trade)—ISBN 978-0-593-37317-0 (lib. bdg.)—
ISBN 978-0-593-37318-7 (ebook)

Printed in the United States of America

10 9 8 7 6 5 4 3 2 1

MARTIN AND CHRIS KRATT: THE WILD LIFE

by Martin Kratt and Chris Kratt
illustrated by Richard Walz

Random House 🏠 New York

Making TV shows is fun,
but making wildlife shows
isn't so easy.

We have been bitten by snakes,
mustelids, a Galapagos shark, and
approximately ten million mosquitoes!

We have been stalked by tigers,
tackled by Komodo dragons,
and charged by elephants.

Hyenas have chewed on our boots—
while we were still wearing them!

We've been lost at sea,
in a rainforest,
and in a desert.

We've carried 200 pounds
of camera equipment
up a mountain,
and then realized
we forgot the film!

Who are we?

We're the Kratt Brothers.

(Yes, we are real brothers!)

I'm Martin, the oldest, and the one in blue.

And I'm Chris, the one in green.

We grew up in a very wild place
called New Jersey.
On our first creature adventures,
we met garter snakes, box turtles,
and toads in the woods behind our house.

As kids, we had normal pets,
like cats and dogs,
and we also liked to learn
about wild animals.

We read books, watched nature videos, and explored the woods whenever we could. We wanted to learn more.

CHRIS

During high school,

I worked at a Raptor Rescue Center

in the Great Swamp near my house.

I loved getting to know hawks,

falcons, eagles and owls.

Then I went to Carleton College
to study biology.
On a field trip to the Boundary Waters
in Minnesota, I saw wolves
in the wild for the first time.

MARTIN

In college, my focus was on zoology, the study of animals. My favorite class was about frogs and salamanders.

I also had a job taking care
of rare lemurs at the Duke Lemur Center.
When I fed the baby aye-aye,
it liked to tap its finger on my watch.

We knew we wanted to help animals, and we wanted to help save endangered species.
We dreamed of telling people about the amazing creatures on the planet by making our own TV show.

It was a long shot, but we had to try.

So we set off into the wild with

a video camera and our backpacks!

First, in Costa Rica, we hiked
to a remote beach to film sea turtles
coming ashore to lay their eggs.
More than twenty thousand turtles
crawled up onto the small beach
as we recorded one night.

It was exciting and a little scary.

Predators like jaguars and crocodiles

also came to the beach,

looking for an easy meal!

We took the video from this adventure and edited it in our parents' basement to make it into wildlife films.
Then we started calling TV stations.

We asked them if they wanted
our show about animals.
Many stations wouldn't even talk to us.
The rest just said "No!"

We were disappointed,
but we wouldn't give up.
Next, we traveled to Madagascar,
the only place in the world where
lemurs—and fossas, tenrecs,
and most chameleon species—
live in the wild.

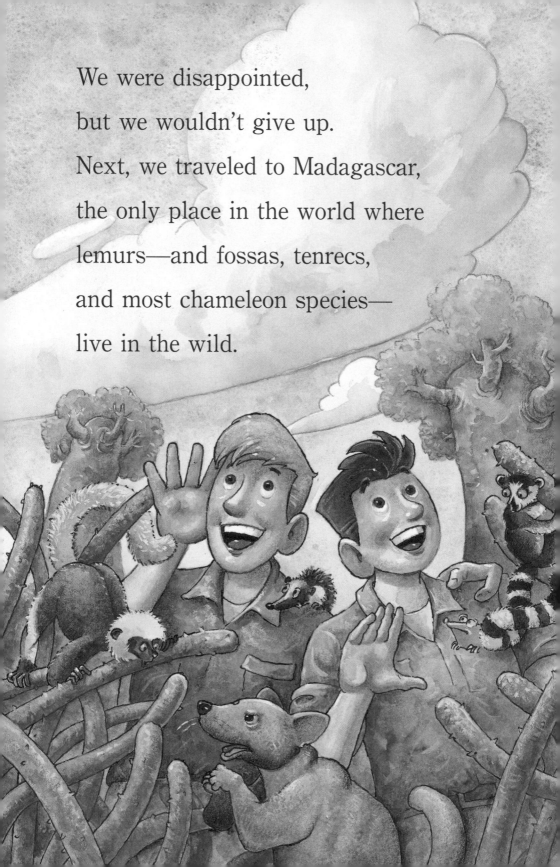

We even filmed the newly discovered
golden bamboo lemur!
Would showing our Madagascar videos
be the key to getting a TV show?

The television people still said "NO."

One producer even said,

"Cute, but it'll never be a TV show."

We decided to keep trying.

So we journeyed deep
into the Amazon jungle
in South America. . . .

One morning, army ants swarmed
into our camp.

They eat everything they come across!

All the animals in the jungle ran
for their lives—and so did we!
We were lucky to get away.

On the lake the next morning,

we were even luckier—

giant otters swam

up next to us!

Giant otters are endangered.
Only a few thousand live in the wild,
and we got to film seven of them!
Then our boat sank, but we
managed to save our video.

We entered that video, *Amazon Adventure,*
in an important film festival.
It won an award!
Our films had gotten better
and better, because we had practiced
by making so many.

The Public Broadcasting System, which most people call PBS, thought our idea was a fun way to learn about animals. It became our very first TV show, *Kratts' Creatures*.

Remembering our time in Madagascar, we made another show, called *Zoboomafoo with the Kratt Brothers.*

It starred
a sifaka lemur
named Zoboomafoo.

All kinds of animals came to visit us and Zoboo in our clubhouse, called Animal Junction.

It was clear to us that animals
have personalities like people.
We went back to the wild to live
with the animals for a new TV show
called *Be the Creature*.

We quickly learned that
"being the creature" isn't easy.
For Komodo dragons, each day can be
a fight for food and resources.
And all creatures use different ways
to survive.

AHHH!

These wild experiences
helped us understand that humans
have many things in common
with wild animals, but that animals
can do things we can't—
they have creature powers!

That thought inspired a new show called *Wild Kratts*. In every episode, we imagine *What if?* and turn into animated versions of ourselves.

As animated characters,
we could run like a cheetah
and swim like a dolphin.

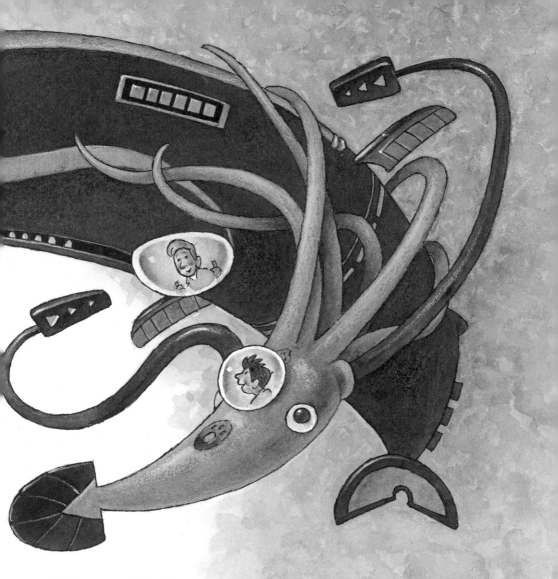

We could show things
that couldn't be filmed in the wild,
such as tardigrades in outer space,
and the battles between colossal squid
and sperm whales in the deep sea.

We started receiving letters and emails
from kids wanting to help animals.
This gave us an idea
for a project to help wildlife.

We would perform live stage shows,

and when kids came to see us,

money would be raised

to protect a wild place

where animals live.

Grizzly Gulch became the first
wildlife refuge created by kid action.
It is a protected habitat
for grizzly bears, wolves, and more.
And we hope to create more refuges
in the future for other wild animals.

CREATURE CAM   05:25AM

CREATURE CAM   12:00AM

03:52PM
CREATURE CAM

It has been a wild journey for us,
with lot of bumps, bruises, and bites.
But there are still lots of
animal species to discover—and we
don't know what will happen next!

Will a snow leopard get into Martin's tent?
Will a bighorn sheep knock over
Chris's camera?
Nature is full of surprises
and new things to discover.
The Kratt Brothers'
creature mission continues. . . .

About the Authors

Brothers Martin Kratt and Chris Kratt
are zoologists by training who have spent
their lives learning about the creature
world and sharing their enthusiasm
for animals. They are actors, directors,
scriptwriters, authors, and wildlife
cinematographers, ever in the pursuit of
"creature adventures."